In the City

By Don Kilby

Kids Can Press

The streets of the city are bustling with people and traffic. Trucks of all shapes and sizes are busy everywhere. Stand at any corner and watch as they rumble past, hard at work.

The **garbage truck** is already on its route as the city wakes up. It pauses at each house while the workers toss in the trash. After a few stops a worker pulls a lever and the truck squishes the load and shoves it deep into the hold. When the truck is full, it drops its load at the depot and then heads back to the street.

By folding in the mirrors and driving very slowly, the driver squeezes the **delivery truck** down the narrow lane to the waiting shopkeeper. From the huge department store in the mall to the tiny corner market, merchants across the city depend on trucks to bring them all the goods they sell. Can you guess what this truck is delivering?

Step right up! This **bus** is off on another trip around the city. There are lots of buses, each traveling a different route, so it's important to be sure you're getting on the right one. Riders let the driver know they want off at their stop by ringing the bell. This bus can carry up to sixty passengers!

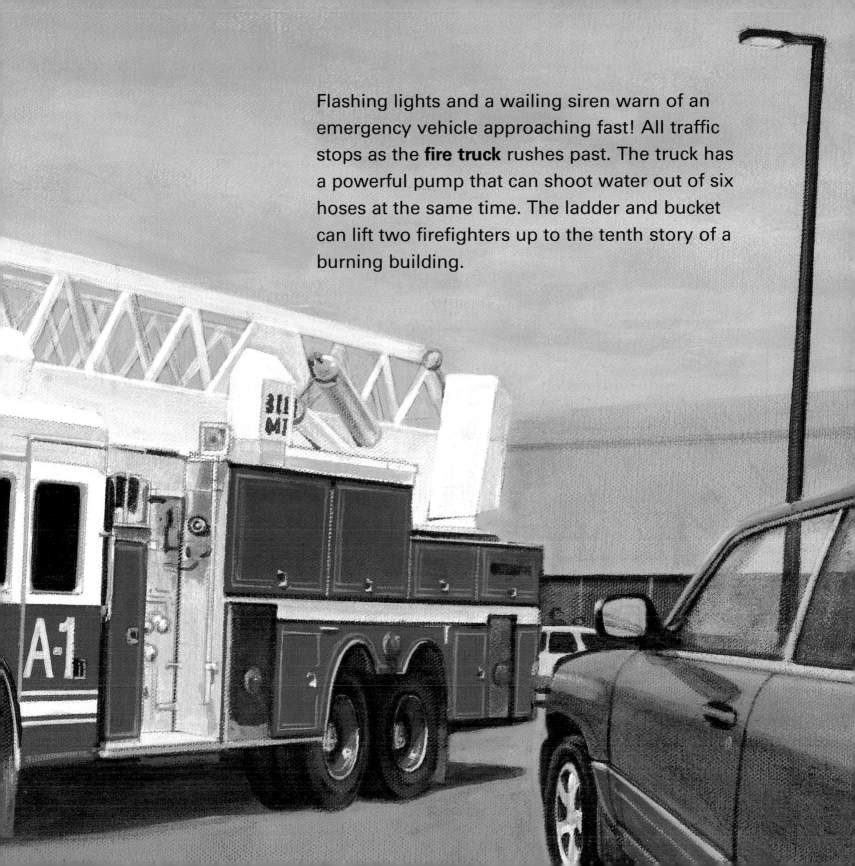

Flashing lights and a wailing siren warn of an emergency vehicle approaching fast! All traffic stops as the **fire truck** rushes past. The truck has a powerful pump that can shoot water out of six hoses at the same time. The ladder and bucket can lift two firefighters up to the tenth story of a burning building.

It's moving day! The workers are busy loading all the family's belongings into the gigantic **moving van**. Everything is carefully packed in and strapped down for the journey to the family's new home.

moving van

Across the street, a **courier truck** stops briefly. The driver rushes out to deliver a package, then hurries away to the next stop.

courier truck

The signal light is broken and traffic is snarled! A police officer keeps things moving while the **bucket truck** lifts a city worker up to make the repair. The machine can be operated from the truck or from inside the bucket. Bucket trucks are also used to trim trees, work on telephone lines and change billboard signs.

chip wagon

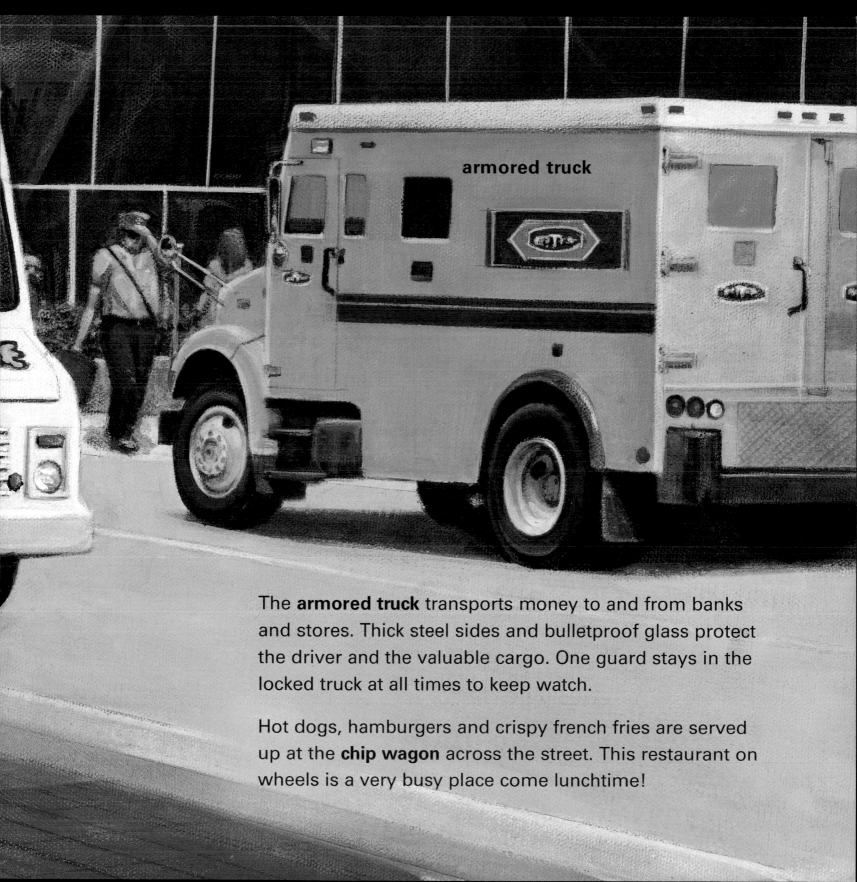

armored truck

The **armored truck** transports money to and from banks and stores. Thick steel sides and bulletproof glass protect the driver and the valuable cargo. One guard stays in the locked truck at all times to keep watch.

Hot dogs, hamburgers and crispy french fries are served up at the **chip wagon** across the street. This restaurant on wheels is a very busy place come lunchtime!

It's not every day you see a **power rodder** at work. Its job is to lay the high-speed communications cables that link our telephones, computers and faxes together. The big drum on the back of the truck acts like a giant fishing reel, pulling the cable slowly through underground pipes.

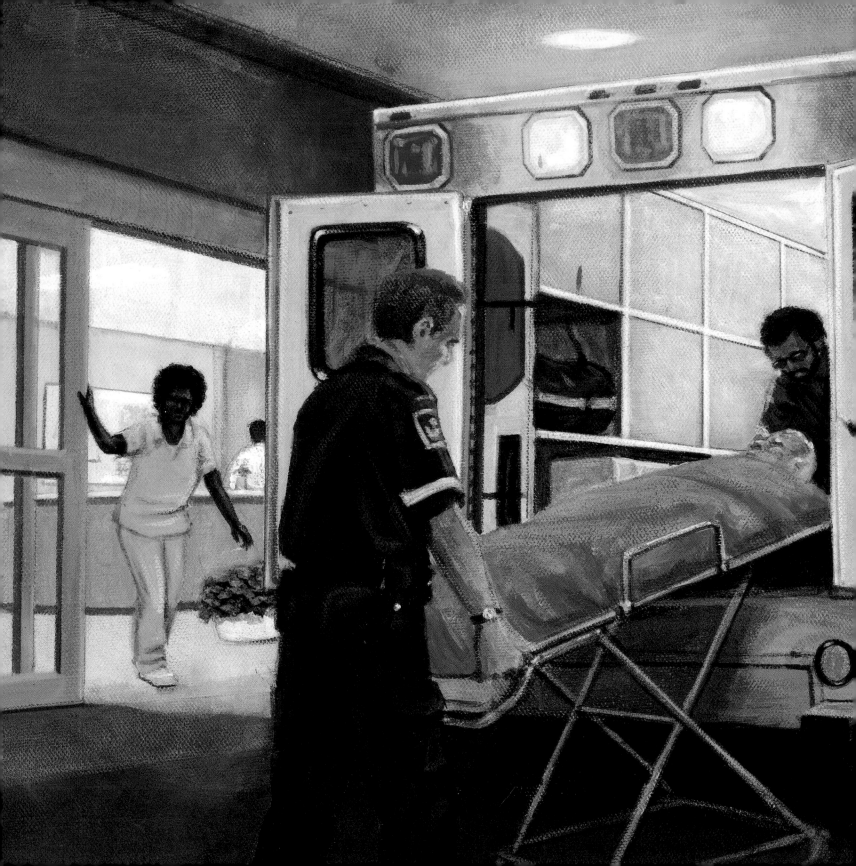

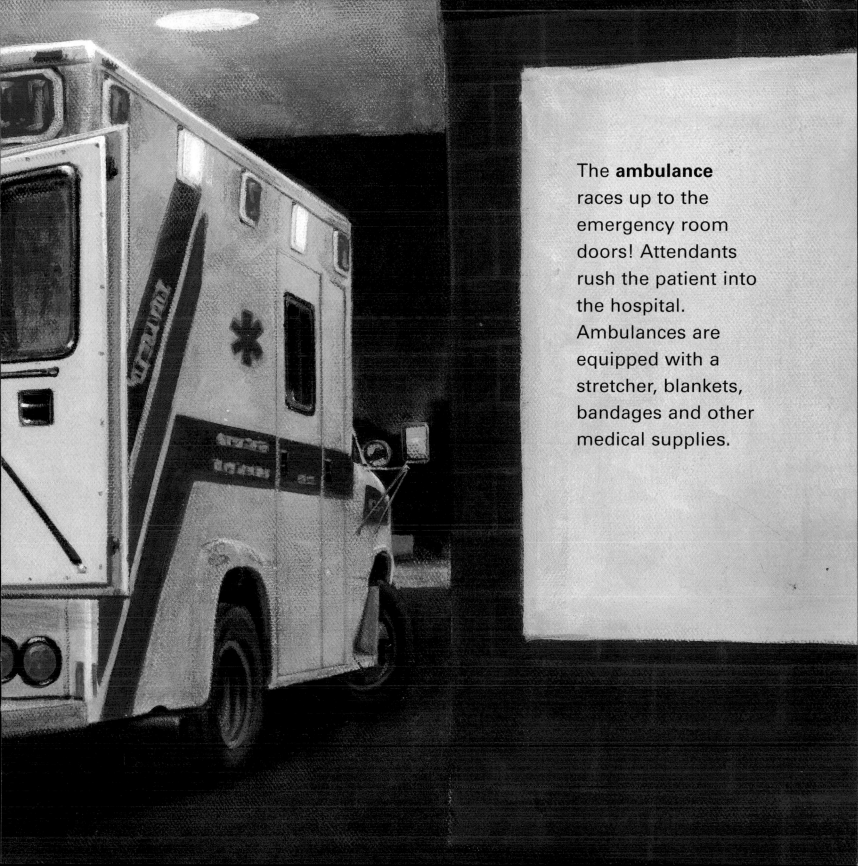

The **ambulance** races up to the emergency room doors! Attendants rush the patient into the hospital. Ambulances are equipped with a stretcher, blankets, bandages and other medical supplies.

The **street sweeper** shuffles by with brushes and scrubbers swirling. Water sprayed from below washes the grit and dust away, leaving the road clean for the start of a new day.

Next time you're out, look around and see how many hardworking trucks you can spot in the city!

To Pat and Joan

Kids Can Press acknowledges the financial support of the Government of Ontario, through the Ontario Media Development Corporation's Ontario Book Initiative; the Ontario Arts Council; the Canada Council for the Arts; and the Government of Canada, through the BPIDP, for our publishing activity.

Published in Canada by	Published in the U.S. by
Kids Can Press Ltd.	Kids Can Press Ltd.
29 Birch Avenue	2250 Military Road
Toronto, ON M4V 1E2	Tonawanda, NY 14150

www.kidscanpress.com

The artwork in this book was rendered in acrylic.
The text is set in Univers.

Edited by Debbie Rogosin
Designed by Marie Bartholomew
Printed and bound in Hong Kong, China, by Book Art Inc., Toronto

This book is smyth sewn casebound.

CM 04 0 9 8 7 6 5 4 3 2 1

National Library of Canada Cataloguing in Publication Data

Kilby, Don
In the city / Don Kilby.

(Wheels at work)
ISBN 1-55337-471-1

1. Motor vehicles — Juvenile literature. 2. Trucks — Juvenile literature. I. Title. II. Series.
TL230.15.K536 2004   j629.22   C2003-905841-7

Kids Can Press is a **Corus**™ Entertainment company